The Overcomer's Life

Living in the Presence of God

Stan E. DeKoven

The Overcomer's Life

ISBN: 978-1-61529-013-0

Copyright © 2009 by Stan E. DeKoven

Published by:

Vision Publishing

1115 D Street

Ramona, CA 92065

www.visionpublishingservices.com

1-800-9-VISION

All scripture references are taken from the NASB version of the Bible unless otherwise noted. Printed in the United States of America

Table of Contents

Introduction

For several years now I have reflected on a nagging question. In Christ, what was, that is, what is history or past, what is, or what is our present reality and what is to come; what remains a future reality in God, from an eschatological perspective.

I suppose it was this question that led me to preach this 2007 Fontana series titled *The Overcomers Life.*

The primary text that I preached this series of messages from was taken from the book of Revelation, chapter 1, verse eight.

> "I am Alpha and the Omega, says the Lord God, who is, who was, and who is to come, the Almighty."

In my initial study of this passage, within the context of John's Revelation of Jesus Christ, I was struck with the lack of proper syntax of the writer; should it not say who was, who is and who is to come? Certainly, that is the way it is sung in our modern choruses. Yet, in keeping with the concept that John was no doubt intentional in his recording of the vision that he received from the Lord, I had to assume the significance of the way he presented this passage of Scripture.

Plus, I approached the series with an expectation of

learning some new things, not just about the life of an Overcomer, but the link between having the perspective of God as a precursor to an overcoming life. So, the study is launched in the order of the passage, beginning with the I AM who is, followed by the I AM who was, and then the I AM who is to come, all of which speaks of God's Almighty power.

Acknowledgments

As in previous editions of the Fontana series, I'm eternally grateful to pastors Gary and Gina Holley of Fontana Christian Center International Fellowship and the congregation with whom they serve Christ, for allowing me the privilege of preaching from behind the sacred desk. They are a blessed, growing congregation with international influence by God's grace. Further, special thanks to some dear friends who've helped me to remain focused on the main thing...God, His presence and purposes. To the following, for so many reasons, I am grateful for their input into my life, their friendship, and for our shared joy in the presence of Christ this work is dedicated to them.

Rev. Laura Allison, Rev. Rob Cunningham, Dr. Jason and Pastor Cathy Guerrero, Rev. Ken Nielsen, Rev. George Runyan, Dr. Kluane Spake, Drs. Joseph and Katherine Thornton, Rev. Ron Wright.

"Trust no Future, howe'er pleasant! Let the dead Past bury its dead! Act-act in the living Present! Heart within and God o'erhead"

Longfellow: A Psalm of Life

The Overcomer's Life: Chapter 1 Who is!

The Priority of His Presence and Reign

Key Scripture: Rev. 1:8, "I am Alpha (Aleph) and the Omega (Taw), says the Lord God, who *is*, and who *was* and who *is to come*, the Almighty."

Preliminary Thoughts

When one thinks of an Overcomer, perhaps a Joni Eareckson Tada, who had a tragic diving accident in 1967, comes to mind. This accident left Joni a quadriplegic in a wheelchair. Today, she is an internationally known mouth artist, a talented vocalist, a radio host, an author of 17 books and an advocate for disabled persons worldwide. In fact, she is an overcomer, but according to scripture all believers' are, at least in one sense, as we have all overcome the world through the blood of Christ and our testimony (Rev. 12:11) and we are more than conquerors in and through Jesus Christ (Rom. 8:37). In fact, our conquering or overcoming is now and always will be in direct proportion to our abiding relationship with Christ. The Almighty one, the true conqueror, lives…and lives in and through us, by His Spirit, according to His marvelous grace, thanks be to God!

A Background

Some history on this phrase would be helpful as we begin our study on this passage of Scripture.

The first usage of this phrase can be found in Isaiah the 41st chapter in the fourth verse as well as in the 44th chapter verse six and 48th chapter and verse 12. In each case the Scripture is speaking of the awesomeness of God and the totality of who he is as our Creator and the sustainer of all that is.

In many ways, this phrase was used as a war chant; designed to, if you will, build up the troops, and also to frighten the enemies of the people of God...for the One who is and was and is to come, The Almighty is with us, and not with you.

He, as the Alpha and the Omega, is the author and the finisher of all things and the sustainer of the universe, and Jesus is the author and finisher of our faith.

Another way of saying this is that God is the aleph and the taw, which are the first and last letters of the Hebrew alphabet, or the beginning and the end of all things, now and forever. In this first chapter my intent is to focus on the order of Jesus' statement here. Again, there is certainly no accident to the words spoken or the order in which they were recorded.

First we see that Jesus is the God who is... he is! One of my favorite songs, sung almost exclusively (if at all anymore) on Easter, is *"He Lives"*. Part of words includes;

> "I serve a risen savior, he's in the world today, I know that He is living, whatever men may say...then the chorus, He Lives, He Lives, Christ Jesus Lives today, He walks with, and talks with me, along life's narrow ways, He Lives, He lives, salvation to impart, you ask me how I know He lives...He lives, within, my heart." Afred H. Ackley Copyright:© 1933 Homer A. Rodeheaver, © Renewed 1961 The Rodeheaver Co. (A Div. of Word, Inc.)

Jesus Christ is alive! It is a true saying that only the fool has said in his heart, there is no God (Psalm 14). It was well stated by Geisler (or at least attributed to him) that in fact he did not have enough faith to believe in no God. True enough, but what does it mean to really believe in, know and experience God's presence? Why is the fact of his very existence and for us his presence, so important? May I suggest that this is so because of what it means to us and the whole world, for we do acknowledge:

- If the light is truly come, then the light of God, which is Christ in the world changes everything in life.

Another way of saying that, what was anticipated is here. From the beginning of time, God in Christ, by the Holy Spirit has been with his creation, from Adam to Abraham to David to now. He is and he has promised his presence with his people.

- That if indeed Christ lives, then those of us who were dead, in our trespasses and sin, really are alive in Christ, and our hope in resurrection is real.

We must remember that at one time we were separated from Christ and destined for dust; we had no hope. We had no hope for the present; we had no hope for the future. Yet in Christ our past, which was unforgivable now is fully forgiven and forgotten.

- But now... Christ is an ever present help in time of need (Ps 46:1).

Thus, we know that he is truly with us at all times in all places where ever we are whatever we do. Further, he is

- He is all powerful; the Almighty is his very name.

As we will look at in chapter 4, God is truly the one who sustains all things by the power of his own word. God is the Creator of all things and through Christ created all that we now see and whatever has been, or ever will be. He is powerful enough to give up life and to take it up again, and give us resurrection life in Christ.

Romans 14 declares;

> "...who has declared the son of God with power by the resurrection from the dead according to the Spirit of holiness, Jesus Christ our Lord."

- He is also purposeful, in that all things are known by God from the beginning.

Job chapter 42:2 rightly states;

> "I know that you can do all things, and that no purposes of yours can be stopped."

- Further, we are a part of God's purposes today, for as believers in Jesus Christ we have been chosen from the foundation of the world to be in him. (Eph. 1:4; 1 Pe. 1:20).

Of course, not only have we been chosen, but God expects us to act as chosen ones. The scripture we recite must become the reality which we live.

- Also Christ is perfect, without flaw, requiring nothing, sovereign over all, yet intimately involved with his creation (Deut 32:4).

This is perhaps one of the most difficult things for the

average believer to actually believe. That is, because we have been cleansed by the blood of Jesus, forgiven from all sin, past, present and future, we have access to his presence every day. Further, who delightful to know that God is not aloof, but is intimately involved with his creation, from the rising of the sun to the setting of the same; we will speak more on this later.

- We also know that because of our relationship with Christ we find that he is Peaceful, but not passive.

Again, we most assuredly should be aware that Jesus is actively involved in his creation. There is much controversy of late regarding just how active Jesus is. The question is, is God all powerful, in the Holy Spirit, to impact and empower the life of the average believer. This is most discussed in reference to God's ability (or lack thereof) to answer prayers. Do we pray simply because we are to do so in obedience, or does prayer really "move the hand of God'?

For most of us, we certainly live as though God does hear and answer our prayers. The reformers, many of which were strongly influenced by Augustinian philosophy, believed in the impassability of God. That is, that God could not be moved in one way or another by the prayers, the need, the problems, the fears or the shouts of pain of his own people. Yet I find within the canon of Scripture ample evidence that God is moved by his people. Our prayers do touch his heart, and God does change his dealings with us according to the obedience that we have toward his word. He is peaceful but he is not passive, and further he is…

- Pastoral, carrying for his children and as his children we are assured from Scripture that God watches over us.

That is not just in a general sense, in that he watches over all of his creation passively, with limited interest. But in fact he watches carefully over his children, showing care and concern about where we are, what we do and how we are living our lives. This is one of the reasons why His presence is to be such an important part of our daily consciousness. That is, as we live our lives, we must do so with a conscious awareness of God's ever present Spirit being with us.

- Not only is he with us but he is passionate for us, for all of his creation, and especially passionate for the lost.

One activity or focus of ministry that is so clearly missing in the Western Church is the zeal to see others come to know Christ as Savior and Lord of their lives. It is a sad commentary on the church in general, but especially on the Western Church. Christ is passionate for the lost. He is not willing that any should perish (2 Peter 3:9) but that all come to righteousness. If we are cognizant of his presence, we will also be cognizant of those men and women in our sphere of influence who have yet to acknowledge Christ as Savior and Lord. The issue is less heaven and hell, though certainly that is a part of the equation, but it is more importantly an issue of life and death. Those that do not know Christ are dead men walking. We have a responsibility as members of the body of Christ to be passionate for what God is passionate about. He is passionate regarding his creation, for as it says in Romans, the whole earth groans for the manifestation of the sons of God. (Rom. 8:19).

My take on that passage is as the Earth continues to be renewed by God's grace and mercy, the whole creation is waiting for God's people to begin to think and act God's way. I am not advocating for the total Christianization of the world. That is certainly not likely to occur. However, the influence of the message of Christ amongst all nations of the world should not only be our goal, but our passion. We are a victorious church! We have been bought with a price. We are a new creation. We are the people of God; kings and priests unto our God, and the whole world is waiting for us to begin to act like it.

- Further, God is our partner in life.

To me that's a very exciting concept. We're not in this world alone, but we have a true partner that walks with us (Immanuel). In the past, many pontificating preachers have prognosticated that Jesus must become our copilot in terms of the management of our life. But in reality, if we're flying the plane, were in the wrong seat. Christ is the pilot and at best, we are the copilot. Yet, God condescends to partner with us because he loves us, may I dare say even likes us, and desires relationship with us as in a partnership for in and for every aspect of life.

- Thus we also know that God is infinitely Patient with our imperfections, our failures, even our foolishness.

Thank God for God's long suffering nature. Because of this, we are always to be grateful for the reality that he has pardoned our many sins, though we are so undeserved. Really, we should be so deeply appreciative. For in fact, we have been marvelously saved by his grace; a grace that makes no sense to the world, so wonderful for us as individual believers. I'm so grateful, most mornings declaring God's word that His mercy is new every morning.

Thus we can persevere; we are able to live and move and have our very existence in him (Acts 17:28) for it has always been his pleasure to give us the keys of the kingdom. (Matt. 16:19) The keys to the kingdom speak about our ability to rule, to function, to be everything God intended for us to be. God's intention is for us to allow his kingdom to rule over every aspect of our life. This is done as we appropriate God's word to our lives, taking his words seriously, and applying it to our lives to the best of our ability as he gives his grace and strength.

Remember, wherever he is, there we are, for we are in him, and he is in us, and where we are, God expresses his pleasure. God is the author of pleasure itself and in his right hand are pleasures forevermore (Ps. 16:11).

Remember we are precious in the sight of our Lord and he sees us not just as his children but really as his very own possession, having purchased this with the blood of his very own son. He is therefore our protector, our high priest, our provider and is the one who prospers us so we can fulfill with faithfulness the purpose for which we were born and born again.

Plus, we should by all means in all situations give him praise, honor, and glory for he is our ever present help; he is with us in all circumstances, and he will never leave us nor forsake us. God is ever present with us. Thus we can boldly go before his throne, to receive mercy and find grace. His presence is not something we must strive for, work up, prey down, or simply attempt to demand. He is, and he is with us because his precious Holy Spirit abides within us. According to Scripture we are seated with Him in the heavenlies. So, where is the heavenlies? Wherever Christ is. And He dwells within us. Thus, in many ways one could say that heaven truly has come to earth, His kingdom has come in the Spirit, and his will is come to earth, and abides in his body, the local church.

God is looking for today is for believers to actually believe. What God is searching for is men and women who will live as though He really was present with them in all things.

In this sense, His light has truly come. His light, His purpose, His desires are readily seen in our individual lives as we live out our purpose where God has placed us.

Now many might ask, how do we appropriate His presence, how do we actualize our potential and purpose in our daily lives? Well, I would like to suggest some key foundational activities that will assist us to connect and or reconnect with the presence of God on a daily basis.

- First of all, there is prayer.

Prayer, as we have all been taught, is simply communicating with God. It includes asking God for things, asking God for others needs, and would include praise and worship. Prayer, sincere, directed, respectful and exuberant prayer should become a daily activity of the everyday believer. Prayer needs to become a fresh focus in the church today.

I am honored to be a part of a leader's prayer group in the community in which I live. This community of leaders is led by a man who is truly passionate for prayer. Pastor George is a man who is dedicated to prayer and to encouraging other leaders to join him in prayer that reduce positive results for God and the city. Because of my frequent out of town trips, I am not always able to meet with my friends in prayer. However, when I'm in town the prayer meeting is a place of rest.

The prayer meeting has also become a place of accountability, in that we must become vulnerable to one another if we're going to be effective in our time of prayer and praise. Of course, nothing compares to the times of personal prayer, devotion, praise, and worship, generally refereed to as our quiet time with the Lord. The prayer closet is something that is desperately needed, and prayer is one of the key ways that we practice the presence of God in our daily life.

- Secondly, it is highly recommended that believers experience the joy of communion or the Eucharist as a key way to connect and reconnect with the presence of God in our lives.

One of the saddest things about the Western church is how little time we spend in remembering what Christ has done, and in remembering one another in the body of Christ. As we break bread, we share intimacy with one another. As we drink of the cup, we're refreshed in our knowledge of what Christ has done for us and our covenant commitment to one another. The Bible says that as often as we do this we do it to remember him. One of the keywords that we miss in this phrase is the word often. That is, we need to do this a lot more often. As we share the elements with one another, we share life. A life must be shared if we are going to grow in love together and thus experience the joy of Christ's presence in our lives.

- Third, is the essential reading and studying of the word of God.

David said your word have I hid in my heart that I might not sin against you. (Ps. 119:11). Jesus said if you abide in my word and my word abides in you, ask whatever you will be done (JN. 8:31). How could Jesus trust his disciples with such a powerful power? Well, he only could if they were truly abiding in him. To abide in Christ is to more than just believe his word, but to actually obey his word. Jesus said if you love me, keep my command (JN. 14:15). Thus, knowledge of God's Word is a real key to developing a deeper intimacy with God, becoming aware of his presence, which is with us at all times.

I would strongly encourage, if you have not begun to do so, you begin today to develop a devotional life. That includes prayer, praise, worship, the word, and deep communion with the Lord and your fellow believers through the breaking of bread.

- Fourth, I must strongly recommend fellowship.

Koinonia or fellowship, as is discussed in Scripture, meant more than just having a potluck dinner together. It really meant sharing life together. In the context of Scripture, Koinonia speaks of a partnership in life, similar to that of marriage, but even more like that of a business partnership. The partnership meant that you were in covenant together, and both were at risk because both brought equal issues or equal investment to the table. We need to recognize, that we desperately need truly committed fellowship or covenantal relationships in the body of Christ.

I remember well the men and women who have influenced my life through preaching and teaching, but I remember most fondly those who, in my darkest days and times came to me and shared their love, grace and kindness with me. In times of my greatest failures, I have had men and women who have said, no matter what Stan, we're going to stand with you. This leads us to the last point, which is…

The importance of true genuine love.

A godly love, sacrificial Godlike love, is hard to find. It's hard to find in any relationship, especially in the body of Christ. For this kind of love requires loyalty, faithfulness, true sacrifice of one's time, talent and treasure, as a relationship is built through the adversities of life over time. When I'm with my friends, those that will hold me accountable, but also will cover my back, are the friendships in which I experience the presence of God most fully. Not just when were involved in religious activity. But on the golf course, over a meal, when were walking the road of life together, these men and women are the ones that remind me of God's wonderful grace, kindness, and compassion (sometimes expressed in tough love).

Each of the activities, for yes, they are actions not just thoughts, are essential for the development of a continuously experienced presence of God. One thing is for certain; God is. And God rewards those who diligently seek Him (He. 11:6).

Our diligent seeking need not be frantic. It should simply be a daily acknowledgment and awareness of his lordship over our lives, and the knowledge that in his presence surely is the fullness of joy. Jesus said I am the Alpha and the Omega, the beginning and the end, the one who is.

I thank God that the one who is, is raining and ruling on his throne of glory, and that we rule and reign with him as his co-heirs of the grace of Almighty God.

Jesus Christ, the same yesterday, today
and forever.

1Sa 15:29 …the Glory of Israel will not lie
or change His mind; for He is not a man
that He should change His mind."

Psa 106:45 "And He remembered His
covenant for their sake, And relented
(repented) according to the greatness of
His lovingkindness."

Jer 18:8, 10 "if that nation against which I
have spoken turns form its evil, I will
relent (repent) concerning the calamity I
planned to bring on it. If it does evil in My
sight by not obeying My voice, then I will
think better for the good with which I had
promised to bless it."

Chapter 2
The Overcomer's Life:
Who Was?

The Creator and Conquering King

To reiterate, it is the very presence of Christ in our lives that is by far the most important thing that we can experience as human beings. But part of experiencing Christ comes out of our knowledge of who Christ was. And this is the area of exploration that we will now take as we look into the nature of Christ, his preexistence as well as his manifestation within Old Testament Scriptures, along with all that he has done for us through his death, burial and resurrection.

I was thinking about several scriptures as I began to meditate on what I would say in this chapter. Several scriptures came to mind.

In Matt 16:13-20 we read;

> "Now when Jesus came into the parts of Caesarea Philippi, he asked his disciples, saying, Who do men say that the Son of man is? And they said, some *say* John the Baptist; some, Elijah; and others, Jeremiah, or one of the prophets. He said to them, But who do you say that I am? And Simon Peter answered; you are the Christ, the

Son of the living God. And Jesus answered and said to him, Blessed are you, Simon Bar-jonah: for flesh and blood did not reveal this to you, but my Father who is in heaven. And I also say to you, you are Peter, and upon this rock I will build my church; and the gates of Hell shall not prevail against it. I will give to you the keys of the kingdom of heaven: and whatsoever you shall bind on earth shall be bound in heaven; and whatsoever you shall loose on earth shall be loosed in heaven. Then he charged the disciples that they should tell no man that he was the Christ."

What a profound question to ask of his disciples; "who do people say that the Son of Man is? Further, the statement of Pilot, and the conversation (if you could call it that) between Jesus and Pilot is so revealing. Pilot asks Jesus the question…

"Are you the king of the Jews?" Jesus response to Pilot was "it is as you say" ("John 18:35-37). Pilot continues in the conversation "I am not a Jew am I? Your own nation and the chief priest delivered you up to me. What have you done? Jesus answered, "My Kingdom is not of this world. If my Kingdom were of this world then my servants would be fighting, that I might not be delivered up to the Jews; but as it is my kingdom is not of this realm. Pilot again said to him "so you are king?" Jesus answered, "you say correctly that I am a king, for this I have been born, and for this I have come into the world, to bear witness to the truth. Everyone who is of the truth here is my voice." Pilate said to him, "what is truth?"

In both of these cases, the identity and mission of Jesus Christ are brought into question, questions are raised that are still germane today.

Especially In the conversation between Pilot and Jesus we see several points that are important to our discussion. First of all, the discussion answers the question that Jesus asked of his disciples. That question again was "who do people say that the Son of Man is?" This is by far one of the most important questions that any human being can ask of themselves, or a question one as a member of our Western culture should ask of one another.

The question really is who is Jesus? Is he just a prophet and/or good teacher, or a man who lived out some positive principles in his generation and time? Is he a guru of some sort, or magician with a magic mojo; really, who is this man called Jesus? This was the question that was on the mind of the disciples in Jesus day, it was a question on the mind of the political and religious leaders of the day. And in many ways, it should be the question upon the minds of people today, within our modern culture. That is, who **is Jesus Christ**?

Let me propose that the chief identity of Jesus Christ, though he is clearly savior, he is the one who sacrificed his life on behalf of others, but most importantly, he is the King of Kings and Lord of lords. We will discuss this more as we go, but it is by far the most important thing for us to remember. Jesus is not just the teacher, prophet, or priest; he is and always has been the King of kings and the Lord of lords.

In John 10:30 Jesus, speaking of himself in relationship to his Father and our Father in heaven makes a profound statement. He says

"I and my Father are one."

Along with this statement, you can link John 14:9, which says

"if you've seen me you have seen the Father."

So, who is this Christ; I mean really, who is he in essence, and why is it vitally important that we know Christ? Here are but a few points for the purpose of our understanding and for further discussion.

I Am Who I Am; I Will Be Who I Will Be

Even as God spoke to Moses from the bush that did not burn up, Jesus Christ is who he is, and will be who he will be. He is the creator of heaven and earth according to the word of God. Several passages of Scripture speak of this to include Genesis 1:26-28; Nehemiah 9:6; Hebrews 11:3; John 1:3. But I want to focus our attention most pointedly on Hebrews Chapter 1:1-4. It reads;

> "God, after he spoke long ago to the fathers in the prophets in many portions and in many ways, in these last days has spoken to us in his son, whom he appointed heir of all things, through whom also he made the world. And he is the radiance of his glory and the exact representation of his nature, and upholds all things by the word of his power. When he had made purification of sins, he sat down at the right hand of the Majesty on high; having become as much better than the angels, as he has inherited a more excellent name than they."

The writer of Hebrews makes a profound statement, that Jesus Christ preexisted all of creation. Jesus is presented as the initiator of the creation of all things. When the Bible says God spoke and light became, it was Jesus who was actually doing the speaking. If you will, the thought was in the Fathers mind, was spoken by the Son and empowered by the Holy Spirit. The trinity of God, the pre-existing trinity of God created all things in and through Jesus Christ the creator. How incredibly powerful Jesus Christ is as the preexisting son of God, who eventually came to earth, to give his life as a ransom for many. He is the creator of all things; how powerful and how marvelous he is.

Further, the Bible says that Jesus is the sustainer of all things. Again, there are many scriptures that speak about the sustaining power of Christ. But according to the power of his own word he keeps everything that is in proper motion. It is difficult if not impossible for us to understand how great and powerful God is in Christ. But we know the one who is and was is the sustainer of all things, from the minutest microscopic particle to the largest black hole in the universe; Jesus Christ sustains it all.

In light of that we see the Jesus Christ is omnipotent; that is, he is all powerful. Many scriptures speak to that reality. It is not just the Father but it's the Son, Jesus Christ who carries all power to be able to do all that is necessary to provide for his children's needs, for their life in God. We will discuss the concept of The Almighty later; suffice it to say that he is all powerful enough to get the job done, whatever the job entails.

Along with being omnipotent, he is omniscient, that is, Jesus Christ as a member of the Godhead knows everything that can possibly be known; how much that is exactly no one fully knows, but we know one thing; he knows everything that needs to be known. The Bible says that the Father even knows the amount of hairs upon her head, and for those of us who have diminishing capacity in terms of our follicle care recognize that for whatever reason he's got a lot of math to do. Simply put, we know that God cares about his creation and he knows all the things that need to be known about his creation and his people, and actively provides for us as his children.

Further, God (Christ) is omnipresent. Jesus Christ is everywhere at all times and especially present with his people as we've already presented. Jesus himself said were two or three gather in his name he is there in the midst of them. We also know that in his preexisted state, prior to the manifestation of Jesus Christ as the son of man born in Bethlehem, raised in Nazareth, etc., that he preexisted as the omnipresent one, being in all places at all times. Of course, this is such a difficult concept for many of us to understand, but one thing we know for certain is that God is with us. Wherever we go he is there, for he dwells in us, with us, so wherever we are there He is. Where He is, there we are, and forever will be, to the glory of God.

Jesus Christ is also the Savior, Lord and King, and is the baptizer in the Holy Spirit. He is the one who has in his earthly ministry modeled for us what it means to be a true God-man.

To complete my thoughts on the Jesus who was, there are a few other scriptures present a clear and dynamic picture of who Christ is, and speaks about a slightly different view of Jesus. All of these scriptures are important to our understanding of the I AM who was.

In 1 Pe.1:18 and 19 Peter writes;

> "knowing that you are not redeemed with perishable things like silver or gold from your futile way of life inherited from your forefathers but with precious blood as a lamb unblemished and spotless the blood of Jesus Christ."

Jesus was crucified from the foundation of the world. Thus stated, we can properly assume that from the beginning of time (or for some, before time was) he had every intention of rescuing us, redeeming us, saving us, healing us, from all that the enemy of our souls would try and rob from us. What we inherited in our natural life were formidable patterns of sin and death. But by the precious blood of Jesus, who came, as it were, as a spotless lamb, a lamb without blemish, a lamb designed to be sacrificed for our benefit, we know that his precious blood has redeemed us, and his plan was to do so from the beginning of time.

In Revelation chapter 1:5 we read,

> "and from Jesus Christ the faithful witness,

the firstborn of the dead, and the ruler of the kings of the earth. To him who loves us, and releases us from our sins by his blood."

Again, just to reiterate, we know that Christ was a faithful witness. All through history, in every manifestation of Jesus in the Old Testament, as an angel, such as the one who visited Jacob, or the one who spoke to Abraham, in every manifestation he was faithful as a witness. Further and more importantly, from the very beginning of time he knew he would be the firstborn of the dead. That is, that resurrection life would lift him from death and that in him all humanity would also have the privilege of experiencing resurrection life in him. He is the ruler of the kings of the earth, whether the kings of the earth acknowledge it or not, he is and he still lives. He is truly the King of Kings and Lord of lords. He is the Second Adam, the one New Man in the earth.

Colossians 1:10 states;

> "for by him all things were created both in the heavens and on earth visible and invisible whether thrones or dominions or rumors or authorities all things have been created by him and for him."

Everything that is and everything that was or ever will be was created and is sustained by our precious Savior, Jesus Christ.

And finally, Jesus came to model what it meant to be like the Father; to be like God in character and purpose. Everything that Jesus did he did so purposefully, from the choosing of his disciples, (see Mark 3) to the parables that he taught, to the life that he lived in terms of how he cared for the needs of others. Everything that Jesus did he did as an example of what it was like to be a God made. As the I AM of God, Jesus demonstrated for each of us exactly what it means to be fully God in every aspect of life. And in and through him we also, by his grace and power can be substantially what Jesus Christ was and is in the world. May God help us as we begin to look now at the one who is to come; the victorious King, our Lord Jesus.

The man who thinks most of the future is generally the man who has no future to think of.

Unknown

Chapter 3
The Overcomer's Life:
Who Is To Come: A Different Jesus
His Purpose Fulfilled

Review of Where We Have Been

Scripture: Rev. 1: 10-20

We began this study with the primary question in mind. What is the priority of God today? Is it the past, with all the glorious history of Israel, and the focus on the death, burial and resurrection of Christ? Is it the future, which we will explore briefly in this section, which speaks about the magnificent, glorious, and dynamic return of Jesus Christ, whether one sees this return as past, soon coming or the distant future? Well, I am certainly not able to properly address these cogent questions in depth in this small booklet. But I will attempt to present what I see as the most important concepts as we look at the future through the eyes and ears of John and his audience, which is where all good biblical study must begin. Of course in looking at the future, we must do so by beginning in the past. The past that I speak of, is that part which is discussed by John the apostle in the book of Revelation beginning with chapter 1 verses 1 to three, and then 10-20.

"The Revelation of Jesus Christ, which God gave

him to show to his bond-servants, the things which must shortly come to pass: and he sent and communicated it by his angel to his bond-servant John; who bore witness to the word of God, and of the testimony of Jesus Christ, *even* of all that he saw. Blessed is he that reads and those that hear the words of the prophecy, and heed the things that are written tin it; for the time is near."

"I came to be in *the* Spirit in the Lord's day and heard behind me a great voice, as of a trumpet, saying, I am the Alpha and Omega, the First and the Last. Also, what you see, write in a book and send *it* to the seven churches which are in Asia: to Ephesus, and to Smyrna, and to Pergamos, and to Thyatira, and to Sardis, and to Philadelphia, and to Laodicea.

And I turned to see the voice that spoke with me. And having turned, I saw seven golden lampstands. And in the midst of the seven lampstands I saw *One* like *the* Son of man, clothed with a garment down to *the* feet, and tied around the breast with a golden band. His head and hair *were* white like wool, as white as snow. And His eyes *were* like a flame of fire. And His feet were like burnished brass having been fired in a furnace. And His voice was like the sound of many waters. And He had seven stars in His right hand, and out of His mouth went a sharp two-edged sword. And His face *was* like the sun shining in its strength.

And when I saw Him, I fell at His feet as dead. And He laid His right hand upon me, saying to me, Do not fear, I am the First and the Last, and the Living One, and I became dead, and behold, I am alive for ever and ever, Amen. And I have the keys of hell and of death. Write the things which you have seen, and the things which are, and the things which shall be after this, the mystery of the seven stars which you saw in My right hand and the seven golden lampstands. The seven stars are the angels of the seven churches, and the seven lampstands which you saw are the seven churches."

The Message Bible States It Like This:

"A revealing of Jesus, the Messiah. God gave it to make plain to his servants what is about to happen. He published and delivered it by Angel to his servant John. And John told everything he saw: God's Word--the witness of Jesus Christ! How blessed the reader! How blessed the hearers and keepers of these oracle words, all the words written in this book! Time is just about up."

"It was Sunday and I was in the Spirit, praying. I heard a loud voice behind me, trumpet-clear and piercing: "Write what you see into a book. Send it to the seven churches: to Ephesus, Smyrna,

Pergamum, Thyatira, Sardis, Philadelphia, Laodicea."

I turned and saw the voice. I saw a gold menorah with seven branches, And in the center, the Son of Man, in a robe and gold breastplate, hair a blizzard of white, Eyes pouring fire-blaze, both feet furnace-fired bronze, His voice a cataract, right hand holding the Seven Stars, His mouth a sharp-biting sword, his face a perigee sun.

I saw this and fainted dead at his feet. His right hand pulled me upright, his voice reassured me: "Don't fear: I am First, I am Last, I'm Alive. I died, but I came to life, and my life is now forever. See these keys in my hand? They open and lock Death's doors, they open and lock Hell's gates. Now write down everything you see: things that are, things about to be. The Seven Stars you saw in my right hand and the seven-branched gold menorah--do you want to know what's behind them? The Seven Stars are the Angels of the seven churches; the menorah's seven branches are the seven churches."

What Revelation Is

For years I read, as perhaps many of you have, the book of the Revelation as primarily a vision or out of body something that John had as a very old and tired man, sometime around 96AD, and that it was all about the yet to come end times. Well, my perspectives have significantly changed over the years. Firstly, thanks to the scholarship of men like Dr. Ken Gentry[1] and others too numerous to mention, I have come to believe that John actually wrote this letter to the actual seven churches of Asia minor before the fall of Jerusalem to the Roman armies under Titus in 70AD. Thus, what John was addressing in the Revelation was not about our times at all, but about those days, and about things that were to shortly come to pass. Further, he was writing to an audience that would have clearly understood the symbols he was using in his writing, symbols that are difficult for us to understand being 2000 years removed from their day and time.

Also, the Revelation was clearly to be shared in those days, as the events to follow in the Revelation were "soon", meaning "soon" to come to pass, not 2000 or more years later.

Finally, as the reader can easily see, the Revelation was not about you, me, America or even Israel, but about our wonderful Lord and Savior, Jesus Christ…in fact, it was and is all about Him.

A Different Jesus

In the 10 - 20 passage of Scripture we see several

---

[1] Gentry, Kenneth, Before Jerusalem Fell, American Vision, Powder Springs, GA, 1998

points that speak about the present reality; specifically that Jesus Christ is the triumphant king. In many ways what is depicted here is what some would see as a different Jesus.

The Jesus that many people know, love and relate to is the meek, mild, gentle, suffering Savior. But the question to be explored in this chapter is, who is the one who we are to worship now, who is come in power and glory, and will come at the end of the time? Further, what we will briefly explore, is what is meant by the end of the age, and what can we anticipate for the future for those of us that are in Christ. Let's look again at some specific points from this passage of Scripture.

First we see that John describes the one to come is the one who is already present in the church. He was present then, and he is present now, and he will always be present with his church. It is essential that we remember at all times that Jesus Christ is the ever present Savior and sustainer keeper of his church. He is in love with the church, his bride, and as one can see in a clear reading of the book of Revelation he comes for his church because he loves it, died for it and stands faithfully with her, desirous of being with his church at all times. Jesus Christ is the head of the church; and we are his body.

A deeper look at the Jesus whom John describes in some detail will help us understand the revelation given. This Jesus described by is no longer meek and mild, but a warrior to be reckoned with. He wears a breastplate, which is indicative of the garb worn by the high priest and also by a King. It demonstrates that Jesus Christ, presently in the church is the high priest of our faith, always living to intercede on our behalf, and he is the King of Kings and Lord of lords. He is pure and regal; he is above all others, worthy to be praised and worshiped.

John further describes him as having white hair which flows as though the wind is rushing through it. In many ways this speaks of the manifestation of the glory of God which was revealed in Christ and continues to be revealed in Christ in our generation. Also, John describes his eyes; his fiery, penetrating eyes that search to and fro in the earth looking for men and women of faith. It would seem impossible to remove oneself from being transfixed on such eyes, as when they look into the soul of a man, empowered by the Holy Spirit, would no doubt be able to burn up sin and bring people into righteousness by the wonderful grace and mercy of God.

We also see Jesus described as one who has a two edged sword coming out of his mouth. In Hebrews chapter 4 verse 12 the word of God says that the word, and the word there means the living Word, is quick and powerful and sharper than even a two-edged sword, which means that he is the overcomer, the one who slays the offender, the one who fights on behalf of his church; the overcoming King, a great, mighty and powerful overlord for the whole world. We also see that his face shines like the sun, again speaking of the glorious King, and the one in whom we have to deal with. He is the one that is to be worshiped. In so many ways we simple human beings are dead men walking. But Jesus is the dead man who is alive forevermore, and gives life to all who believe.

The Bible indicates that Jesus will rule and reign from his throne in heaven, through his church until every enemy is made of footstool and until the earth is covered with the knowledge of the glory of the Lord as the waters cover the sea. The last enemy is death.

From a spiritual view, death has been clearly defeated in Jesus Christ, and Satan's power destroyed. As Paul declared, Death where is your victory, grave where is your sting? The fact is that Jesus Christ did triumph over death, hell and the grave, and we are more than conquerors through Jesus Christ. His conquering will continue, as will his Kingdom be without end.

So, what was Jesus talking about when he referred to the end of the age in response the questions of his disciples? (Mat. 24:3) Well without going into a deep study let me share with you some y thoughts that bring us up to our present time.

First, the end of the age speaks mainly of the end of

the old covenant era. Jesus said in Matthew 24 and other references, that this generation, the generation in which he lived, would not pass away until all the prophecies he spoke of would be fulfilled. In 70 A.D., judgment came upon the apostate Jews, as Jesus prophesied would occur, and the kingdom was fully transferred from Israel in its natural state to the Israel of God, which is the church. At that point, all that needed to be done, had been, to usher in the marvelous kingdom age in which we now live.

So many would say what now? What do we have yet to look forward to? Well let me put it this way. Not much and the most exciting times the church has ever seen. What we are commissioned to do in our day and time is to continue the enforcement of the rule of the King until every nation has had opportunity to hear the gospel of Jesus Christ, and where every nation under the sun would have opportunity to hear the good news of Christ, and either repent and come into the rest of God, or perish. So what is required of the people of God today? Well, to preach the gospel of the kingdom of course. And for how long will we continue to this? Until every enemy has been defeated and until all nations have heard the good news of Jesus Christ. How long will that take? Only God knows.

What I know is that Jesus Christ is the present ruling king. And we his people are seated in the heavenlies with Christ! He is far above every principality and power and worker of darkness, and we enjoy the bird's eye view of the Kingdom as well. The Bible clearly states that Satan is under our feet. He is a defeated foe. And we stand, presently triumphant in his presence! What God intends for us today is to live out our life as ambassadors for Christ as members of the kingdom of God, as priest and kings before God, until all that God intends to happen has been fulfilled.

In many ways we live in one of the most exciting eras of all-time. I am certain there will continue to be a strong emphasis on the present church being the last generation; we are in the end times. But of course, as Peter said on the first day of the church in acts chapter 2 in the last days God would pour out his Spirit on all flesh. He has; he is and he will continue to pour out his Spirit on all flash until everything that must be fulfilled, for the earth will be covered with the knowledge of the glory of the Lord as the waters cover the see. May God continue to pour out his blessings on his glorious church, for the healing of the nations.

If the whole universe has no meaning, we should never have found out that it has no meaning: just as, if there were no light in the universe and therefore no creatures with eyes, we should never know it was dark. Dark would be without meaning.

C. S. Lewis

Chapter 4
The Overcomer's Life:
The Almighty One

There is an old old chorus that says "how great is our God, how great is his name, he is the greatest one, for ever the same. For he rolled back the waters of the mighty red sea, and he said I'll never leave you, put your trust in me."

With certainty, and in absolute terms, the Bible offers to us a God that is above all others, greater than any rival, and more. Of course, philosophers and theologians have debated his absoluteness or omniscience, omnipresence and omnipotence, especially the latter, for generations. Both in the church and without, usually found in dialog regarding the most difficult topic of suffering and injustice in the world, have asked the question if God is really all powerful, why does he allow in justice, injury, suffering especially amongst the innocents, the most innocent of all being children, to continue in the world? God either must not be good, because he allows such things or God is not all-powerful, all mighty. Another ways of stating this is would not a truly good God change the injustices of the world and alleviate human suffering? Or some might also state, that God is good, and wants his creation to be happy, but he is just not able to make it so. That is to say, though God is good, and in his good intentions he wants to bless, prosper and protect his children fully, he just doesn't have all the power that many people say that he does.

Well, many better minds than mine have and continue to debate this important subject.[2] In the appendix of this small book, I have provided a listing of some resources to help the serious student grapple with this very important topic, along with others germane to this booklet. For our benefit, I will choose to affirm what I believe is a reasonable, biblical self-assessment, with commentary on God's power; His unlimitedness and limits.

The Almighty: Meaning and References

There are numerous references or usages of the title and the term All Mighty(54 or so in total) as both a title and attribute of God. I have selected several for consideration and discussion. But first, a couple of definitions.

The primary word for Almighty used in the Old Testament is the word *Shadday*. One of the primary meanings of this word as related to the Lord is the God who supplies or, as revealed to Abraham, the God who is Provider, Shelter, Giver, Life, Sufficient, and all Abraham needed.[3] In the New Testament, the

---

[2] *Walking with a Limp: A Charismatic Approach to Suffering Adelaide*: Open Book, 2002.
[3] *Who is God* by Harold Eberle, Worldcast Publishing, Yakima, WA 2009.

Almighty is the Sovereign, (*Pantokrator*) or the all ruling one...Lord of all. Certainly, we know that the Lord, who knows the number of diminishing hairs on our heads has intimate knowledge of who we are and what we need (Matt. 10:30).

Yet, an ongoing question remains does he really know all details of all things (and does that matter) and if not, what does he know, does he ever change his mind, etc. Anyway, here are some scriptures to think on.

Gen 17: And when Abram was ninety years old and nine, Jehovah appeared to Abram, and said unto him, I am God Almighty; walk before me, and be perfect.

Gen 35:11 And God said unto him, I am God Almighty: be fruitful and multiply; a nation and a company of nations I will make of you, and kings shall come out of your loins;

Exo 6:3 and I appeared unto Abraham, unto Isaac, and unto Jacob, as God Almighty; but by my name Jehovah I was not known to them

Job 5:17 Behold, how happy is the man whom God reproves, So do not despise the discipline of the Almighty.

Ps 91:1 He that dwells in the secret place of the

Most High Shall abide under the shadow of the Almighty.

Rev 11:17 saying, We give thee thanks, O Lord God, the Almighty, who is and who was; because you have taken you great power, and reign.

Mal 3:6, I, the Lord, do not change…

Amos 7:6…the Lord changed his mind

Heb 13: 8 Jesus Christ, the same yesterday, today and forever.

I appreciate the perspective presented by Dr. Ken Chant from his book Attributes of Splendour[4] in discussing God's all powerfulness. He states;

> "What can he (God) do? "Anything he pleases!" –whether in heaven or on earth (Ps 135:5-7). That is, God is limited only by his own choice and character; no boundary nor restraint can be placed upon his actions save those that are…inherent in his nature…determined by his will…and logically inconsistent."

So, what is his nature? Well, in short, God is love, and in his love he is omniscient, that is he knows all that is knowable, though there is much dispute

[4] Chant, Ken, *Attributes of Splendour,* Vision Publishing, Ramona, CA 2007.

regarding if he knows the future…but all possibilities leading to the future would clearly be known by God. Further, he is omnipresent, by his Spirit, living in all who know him, ready to respond to the hint of pray from a penitent sinner. He is just, he is merciful, he is judge…he is good.

What has he determined to be his will? Well, we know that he wills that no one parish, but the fact remains that countless thousands likely will, by their own choosing, or no choosing when confronted with the gospel of the Kingdom, to respond in repentance and acceptance of his rule in their lives. Thus, many sadly will perish, in spite what the Lord wills. He wills that we be conformed to his image, but again, how many believers consistently manifest the fruit of the Holy Spirit in their daily walk?

His will is to reconcile all men to himself, to see his Kingdom expanded to its fullest expression…all of which seems to be possible only with the cooperation of man, a limitation on the all powerfulness of God, even if self limited.

Finally, what is logically consistent to us mere mortals is not necessarily so to God. Isaiah 55: 8 reminds us;

> "For My thoughts are not your thoughts, neither are your ways my ways, declares the Lord."

Some Final Thoughts

In conclusion, we again asked the question what is past, what is present, and what is future. Or another way of saying it is, what is, what was, and what is to come as members of the glorious church of Jesus Christ. Here in final thoughts is a brief summary.

In Christ, what was is all that we ever see today. God is the creator and sustainer of life, having done so through the word of Jesus Christ who is the living Word. What was includes God's covenant with us his people, and with all mankind to an extent, but especially the covenant of Abraham. We who know Jesus Christ as Savior and Lord are the beneficiaries of or inheritors of this glorious and comprehensive. What was is that Jesus came, in human flesh, lived a sinless, perfect life and died on the cross, according to the foreknowledge of God, rising again on the third day from the dead, and is presently seated at the right hand of the Father in power, glory and majesty.

In Christ what is now? Well now is the day of salvation. Now all are living under the Lordship of Christ, whether this is known and accepted or not. Now we are a new creation. Now we know that Christ has provided to us complete victory, a full salvation, sanctification, glorification; all things necessary for life and godliness, has been provided to us in Christ. We can and should experience the benefits of our relationship with Christ right now.

Jesus Christ, by the Holy Spirit living in us, is ever present with us. In his presence is the fullness of joy and the joy of the Lord is our strength. In Christ, right now, we have a completed identity. We can know who we are because we know who's we are. We belong to Jesus. And he has for us life and health and strength and purpose and healing and grace and mercy and the fruit of the Holy Spirit and eternal life through Jesus Christ...Hallelujah!

And what is to come? In the 70 A.D. world in which we, the covenant people of God live, what is it that we should expect? We should expect to see a glorious church, a victorious church, a triumphant Church, were all of the enemies of the Lord eventually become his footstool. Right now and for the future, Jesus Christ is the Lion of the tribe of Judah, and we are kings and priests with our Lord in the present. Plus, we are called to enforce a victory that has been won through the cross of Christ, and a one gained as we live life to the fullest, motivated and guided by agape. Thus God intends for us to take up the sword of the Spirit, which is the word of God, being motivated by the love of God, and do the works that Jesus came to do, and even greater works, because he is gone to be with the Father, and is seated at his right hand. Of course, in the church today we need to learn to love one another, as we grow from glory to glory and from strength to strength.

So what is yet to come? More of the same and even

better. A church expanding, growing and changing things in spite of what we may see, until the Lord sees fit to say it is done.

It is my hope that as you have read this little booklet that your focus has been on the main thing...the wonderful presence of God. One of my greatest joys in life and ministry is sharing with other men and women of like passion the presence and power of our risen Christ. I am especially blessed when we come together, at the Table of the Lord, and express the love of Christ in each of us for one another, and enjoy afresh the wonderful presence of Jesus.

The overriding reason to be in his presence is to worship him, to receive instruction, so that we can be the salt and light in the world as Christ commanded. God has, through Christ, redeemed the world that he died for. He wants every man, woman and child to experience his love, his grace, his life. For whatever reason, God has chosen to work with us, his children, to bring about his great purposes. I will never know exactly what John saw on the island of Patmos; anyone who says he or she does is delusional. What we do know is that experiencing the risen Christ, the one who is, and was and is to come, The Almighty, changed him. He recognized that God who is Christ Jesus is powerful, is capable, and when his church allows themselves to be filled with God's Spirit, can and will be more than conquerors, triumphant to the glory of God. He has called us to be men and women whose hearts and minds are fully transformed by the power of God's love, his mercy and his marvelous grace.

Other Books by the Author

Assessment in Counseling
Christian Education
Crisis Counseling
Family Violence
40 Days to the Promise
Fresh Manna
From A Father's Heart
Grief Relief
Healing Community
Homiletics
I Want to be Like You Dad
Journey Through the New Testament
Journey Through the Old Testament
Journey to Wholeness
Living Fruitfully
Marriage and Family Life
New Beginnings
On Belay!
Parenting on Purpose
Pastoral Ministry
Prelude to a Requiem
Research Writing Made Easy
Strategic Church Administration
Supernatural Architecture
That's the Kingdom of God
Transferring the Vision
Twelve Steps to Wholeness
Visionary Leadership